THE OUTDOORS
BOWHUNTING
by Tyler Omoth

FOCUS READERS

FOCUS READERS

WWW.FOCUSREADERS.COM

Focus Readers is distributed by North Star Editions:
sales@northstareditions.com | 888-417-0195

Produced for Focus Readers by Red Line Editorial.

Photographs ©: DLCcreates/iStockphoto, cover, 1; ViktorCap/iStockphoto, 4–5; W. Scott McGill/Shutterstock Images, 6; Yermolov/Shutterstock Images, 8–9; spxChrome/iStockphoto, 10; HildeAnna/iStockphoto, 12; gopher777/iStockphoto, 14 (top left); sb-borg/iStockphoto, 14 (top right); Jeffrey B. Banke/Shutterstock Images, 14 (bottom left), 14 (bottom right), 25; MidwestWilderness/iStockphoto, 15 (top left); xp3rt5/iStockphoto, 15 (top right); quadshock/Shutterstock Images, 15 (bottom left); beachnet/iStockphoto, 15 (bottom right); loonger/iStockphoto, 16–17; Jeff Lampe/Peoria Journal Star/AP Images, 19; Bruce MacQueen/Shutterstock Images, 21; Windzepher/iStockphoto, 22–23; NaturesMomentsuk/Shutterstock Images, 26–27; Jonathon Pryor/Shutterstock Images, 28

ISBN
978-1-63517-225-6 (hardcover)
978-1-63517-290-4 (paperback)
978-1-63517-420-5 (ebook pdf)
978-1-63517-355-0 (hosted ebook)

Library of Congress Control Number: 2017935876

Printed in the United States of America
Mankato, MN
June, 2017

ABOUT THE AUTHOR

Tyler Omoth is the author of more than two dozen books for children on topics ranging from baseball to Stonehenge to turkey hunting. He loves going to sporting events and taking in the sun at the beach. Omoth lives in sunny Brandon, Florida, with his wife.

TABLE OF CONTENTS

CHAPTER 1

Up for the Challenge 5

CHAPTER 2

Bowhunting Basics 9

EQUIPMENT CHECKLIST

Bowhunting Supplies 14

CHAPTER 3

Before the Hunt 17

CHAPTER 4

Safety Tips 23

CHAPTER 5

Respecting Nature 27

Focus on Bowhunting • 30
Glossary • 31
To Learn More • 32
Index • 32

UP FOR THE CHALLENGE

You sit motionless in your tree stand. You blow on a call, making a low grunting noise. Then your eyes catch motion. You **draw** your bow as a white-tailed deer walks toward you. You aim carefully and release the string. The arrow zips through the air and hits its mark. It's a perfect shot!

Shooting arrows with a bow is sometimes called archery.

Early arrowheads were often made from stone such as flint.

Bows were invented thousands of years ago. People shaped flexible pieces of wood into bows. They fitted the bows with strings. Bows allowed people to fire arrows at any target. Hunters no longer had to get close enough to an animal to throw a spear. They could hunt animals without putting themselves in as much danger.

When hunting rifles were developed in the 1800s, bowhunting was no longer necessary. But many people still enjoyed the challenge of hunting with bows and arrows. Early arrows were made of wood. But in 1939, aluminum arrows were introduced. These metal arrows were stronger and lighter. People also invented stronger bows. The first compound bow was created in 1966. It used a series of **pulleys**. This made it possible for hunters to shoot farther and with more force than ever before. Every year, millions of people take to the woods to bowhunt.

CHAPTER 2

BOWHUNTING BASICS

Bowhunters enjoy hunting a wide variety of animals. Deer, elk, and moose are popular targets. Other hunters pursue mountain goats or turkeys. Some bowhunters even shoot bears.

Hunters carry their arrows in a container called a quiver. Arrow tips used for hunting are called broadheads.

Wearing camouflage clothing helps hunters blend in with their surroundings.

A broadhead arrow tip is extremely sharp.

Broadheads are larger than the arrow tips used by archers who shoot at targets. Their sharp points help hunters make clean kills.

A traditional bow uses a string attached to a frame. The frame is made from flexible material such as wood. As the hunter draws the bowstring back, the bow's frame flexes. This adds pressure to the string. When the hunter releases the string, the pressure is released, too. This sends the arrow forward.

Some hunters use compound bows. A compound bow's pulleys make it easier for the hunter to pull back the string. The pulleys also increase the **thrust** of the arrow. As a result, hunters who use compound bows can shoot game from farther away. They can also take down bigger animals.

Some hunters carry their tree stands on their backs.

Tree stands help bowhunters get good shots. Hunters set up tree stands near areas where animals often come. Being up in a stand gives the hunter a clear line of sight. The view from a tree stand should always be free of branches that could block the shot.

Hunters may use lure scents to bring animals closer to their stands. They may also use cover scents to make sure animals will not smell them.

Binoculars help hunters see animals that are far away. A hunting knife is a useful tool that every hunter should carry as well.

GAME CALLS

One of the best ways to lure game closer is to use a call. Each type of animal has several different calls. Some calls are loud and aggressive. Others are soft. By learning the different calls and when to use them, hunters can bring in their game for a great shot.

BOWHUNTING SUPPLIES

☐ 1. Arrows

☐ 2. Binoculars

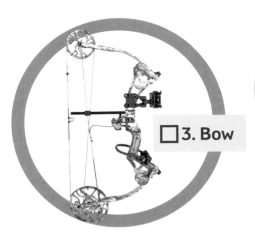

☐ 3. Bow

☐ 4. Extra broadheads

☐ 5. Game call

☐ 6. Hunting knife

☐ 7. Quiver

☐ 8. Tree stand

CHAPTER 3

BEFORE THE HUNT

Bowhunting requires patience and a lot of practice. Hunting with a bow can be more difficult than hunting with a gun for several reasons. Bows are not as powerful as guns. They are less accurate at long distances. Because of these limitations, it is important for bowhunters to aim carefully.

People often practice their shooting skills at archery ranges.

A bow's draw weight is important. The draw weight is the amount of pressure needed to pull back the bow's string. The harder it is to draw the string, the more power the shot will have.

Hunters should choose the correct draw weight based on the type of animal they are hunting. Some areas have laws

ARCHERY RANGES

At archery ranges, hunters practice shooting a bow and aiming for targets. Some hunters use targets shaped like deer, bears, or other animals. These three-dimensional targets help hunters practice shots that will make a clean kill. Hunters learn the best places to aim for each kind of animal.

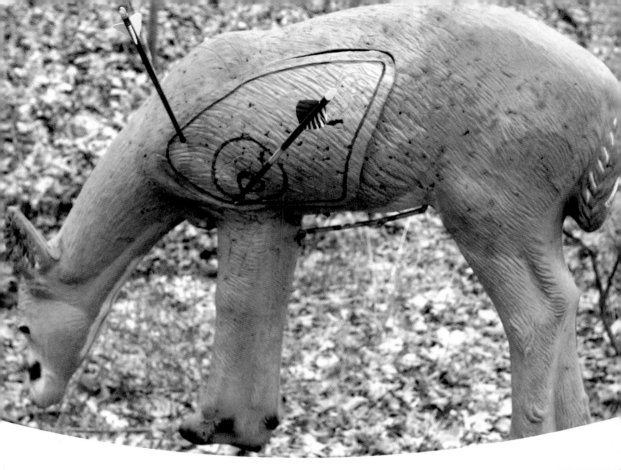

Targets shaped like animals help hunters practice their aim before the hunt.

that declare a minimum draw weight. Each hunter should make sure that his or her bow is up to the task. A bow that is too weak may injure an animal without making a clean kill.

A shot to the heart or lungs of an animal is the surest way to get a clean kill. For most four-legged animals, such as deer or bears, a hunter should aim just behind the animal's shoulder. But each animal has a slightly different **anatomy**. Hunters study the best kill shots for each kind of animal they hunt.

Hunters should also look for potential hunting areas before the season begins. When **scouting**, hunters look for an area where there are many animals. It can be hard to see the animals themselves, so hunters often look for signs of animal activity. Footprints, clearly worn paths, and **scat** show that animals are nearby.

Matted grass and flattened leaves are common signs of deer beds, or places where deer have lain down.

Large, flattened patches of grass may show that animals use the area for resting.

Some signs indicate the presence of particular animals. For example, deer and elk scrape their antlers on trees. This creates obvious marks. Bears also claw at trees to mark their territory.

CHAPTER 4

SAFETY TIPS

When a bow's string is released, it can snap along the hunter's arm. To prevent injuries, a hunter should wear an arm guard. This protective sleeve goes on the hunter's extended arm. The string can also sting the hunter's fingers. Because of this, many hunters wear archery gloves.

Many archery gloves have only three fingers.

Leather guards on the gloves' fingers protect hunters' hands.

The arrows used for hunting are extremely sharp. They should never be carried loose or **nocked** in a bow. Instead, hunters should store their arrows in a quiver. They should keep the quiver's top closed until they are ready to shoot.

Climbing into a tree stand while carrying a bow and quiver is dangerous. Instead, hunters should use a rope to pull up the bow and quiver after them.

Each hunter in a tree stand should wear a safety harness, too. The harness secures the hunter to the tree and helps prevent falls.

A hunter pulls up his bow with a rope.

CHAPTER 5

RESPECTING NATURE

Each area has its own hunting seasons and regulations. Governments make these laws to protect animals. Hunting seasons vary for different **species** of animals. Bowhunters should learn and follow the laws for the kinds of animals they plan to hunt. Bowhunters must also buy the appropriate hunting licenses.

Some programs that protect wildlife get their funding from license sales.

Hunters look for footprints to track a wounded animal.

Money from license sales is used to **preserve** the animals' **habitats**.

Hunters should respect natural areas during the hunt. They should not leave anything behind at their hunting site. This includes arrows. Fired arrows can be hard to find. But hunters should never leave them out in the woods. Hunters should also track down any animals they shoot.

Bowhunting is an activity that has survived for thousands of years. By following hunting guidelines, bowhunters help make sure that this thrilling activity will be around for many more.

TRACKING AN ANIMAL

Hunters must be careful when tracking a wounded animal. They should always be prepared to find cover in case there are other animals nearby that could attack. Hunters should be careful when they find the animal, too. An animal with its eyes closed is likely still alive. It could still injure the hunter.

FOCUS ON
BOWHUNTING

Write your answers on a separate piece of paper.

1. Write a letter to a friend describing the main ideas of Chapter 4.

2. Why do you think people continued to hunt with bows after rifles were invented?

3. How is a compound bow different from a regular bow?
   - **A.** A compound bow uses a set of pulleys.
   - **B.** A compound bow fires arrows from four strings at once.
   - **C.** A compound bow has more than one frame.

4. Why would a tree stand help a bowhunter get a good shot?
   - **A.** It blocks noises that could distract the hunter.
   - **B.** It helps the hunter focus on a smaller area.
   - **C.** It lifts the hunter above bushes and branches.

Answer key on page 32.

GLOSSARY

anatomy
The physical structure of a living thing.

draw
To pull back the string on a bow.

habitats
The type of places where plants or animals normally grow or live.

nocked
When an arrow is fitted to the bowstring in preparation for shooting.

preserve
To protect something so that it does not change.

pulleys
Wheels with grooves that a rope or chain runs through.

scat
The waste of an animal.

scouting
Looking for signs of animals.

species
A group of animals or plants that are similar.

thrust
The forward force of a launched object.

TO LEARN MORE

BOOKS

Frazel, Ellen. *Bow Hunting*. Minneapolis: Bellwether Media, 2013.

Hemstock, Annie Wendt. *Bow Hunting*. New York: PowerKids Press, 2015.

Howard, Melanie A. *Bowhunting for Kids*. North Mankato, MN: Capstone Press, 2012.

NOTE TO EDUCATORS

Visit **www.focusreaders.com** to find lesson plans, activities, links, and other resources related to this title.

INDEX

archery gloves, 23–24
archery ranges, 18
arm guard, 23
arrows, 5–7, 9–11, 24, 28

binoculars, 13
broadheads, 9–10

calls, 5, 13
compound bow, 7, 11
cover scents, 13

draw weight, 18–19

hunting licenses, 27–28

lure scents, 13

quiver, 9, 24

safety harness, 24
scouting, 20

tracking, 29
tree stands, 5, 12, 24

Answer Key: 1. Answers will vary; **2.** Answers will vary; **3.** A; **4.** C